Brief Summary of the Technical Feasibility Emissions, and Fuel Economy of Pure Methanol Engines

U.S. Environmental Protection Agency

The BiblioGov Project is an effort to expand awareness of the public documents and records of the U.S. Government via print publications. In broadening the public understanding of government and its work, an enlightened democracy can grow and prosper. Ranging from historic Congressional Bills to the most recent Budget of the United States Government, the BiblioGov Project spans a wealth of government information. These works are now made available through an environmentally friendly, print-on-demand basis, using only what is necessary to meet the required demands of an interested public. We invite you to learn of the records of the U.S. Government, heightening the knowledge and debate that can lead from such publications.

Included are the following Collections:

Budget of The United States Government
Presidential Documents
United States Code
Education Reports from ERIC
GAO Reports
History of Bills
House Rules and Manual
Public and Private Laws

Code of Federal Regulations
Congressional Documents
Economic Indicators
Federal Register
Government Manuals
House Journal
Privacy act Issuances
Statutes at Large

EPA-AA-SDSB-82-1

Technical Report

A Brief Summary of the Technical Feasibility,
Emissions and Fuel Economy of
Pure Methanol Engines

by

Jeff Alson

December 1981

NOTICE

Technical Reports do not necessarily represent final EPA decisions
or positions. They are intended to present technical analysis of
issues using data which are currently available. The purpose in
the release of such reports is to facilitate the exchange of technical information and to inform the public of technical develop-
ments which may form the basis for a final EPA decision, position
or regulatory action.

Standards Development and Support Branch
Emission Control Technology Division
Office of Mobile Source Air Pollution Control
Office of Air, Noise and Radiation
U.S. Environmental Protection Agency

I. Introduction

Because of the general perception that our country cannot afford to continue to rely on foreign sources for nearly half of our petroleum supply, considerable resources both in the private and public sectors are being expended to develop alternative liquid fuels which could power future automotive vehicles. Fuels under consideration include alcohol fuels such as methanol, which can be synthesized from coal, natural gas, wood or other biomass feedstocks, and ethanol, which is produced by the fermentation of sugars and starches, as well as synthetic gasolines, diesel fuels, and broad-cut fuels from coal and oil shale. Because of their strong dependency on fuel type, the environmental and energy characteristics of the various alternative fuels are of primary concern. Clearly, the emissions and efficiency capabilities of the various alternative fuels, which often have very different physical and chemical properties, should be important determinants in the selections of acceptable alternative fuels.

This report deals with just one of the fuels under study -- methanol. In the last decade considerable research has been undertaken to evaluate methanol as an automotive fuel and this report will attempt to summarize the emissions and fuel efficiency data from the many studies. Because there is a general consensus that pure methanol is preferable to methanol/gasoline or methanol/diesel fuel blends (as opposed to ethanol which is very satis-factory in blends such as gasohol), and because the emissions and efficiencies of vehicles operating on pure methanol are sometimes much different from those operating on methanol blends, this paper will generally limit itself to data involving pure methanol combustion. A notable exception will be the sections dealing with methanol combustion in compression-ignited diesel engines. Because of the paucity of data on pure methanol combustion in such engines, much of the data will involve the use of pilot fuels (to aid ignition) in addition to methanol.

The first section of this report will consider the important physical and chemical properties of methanol which define its characteristics as a motor fuel, and will compare its properties to those of gasoline and diesel fuels. The report will then briefly summarize the state-of-the-art of the technical feasibility of pure methanol vehicles. Next, it will examine the emissions of various pollutants from methanol-fueled vehicles, both in terms of what would be theoretically expected and what has been experimentally determined. Finally, it will summarize the fuel efficiency results of studies of methanol-fueled vehicles.

Recent motor vehicles have utilized internal combustion engines which can be divided into two general groups. One group of engines combust a homogeneous mixture with a precisely controlled air/fuel mixture, utilizing throttled intake air, fuel induction, and spark ignition, and generally utilizing gasoline as fuel. A second group of engines combust a heterogeneous mixture containing excess air at high compression, utilizing direct-cylinder fuel injection and compression ignition, and generally utilizing diesel fuel. These two engine types are often referred to as spark-ignited and compression-ignited engines, or, more popularly outside the industry, as "gasoline" and "diesel" engines. The distinctions between these two engine types have blurred in recent years, however, as engines have been developed which utilize characteristics of both engine types. For example, stratified-charge engines (such as Ford's PROCO) combust a hetero-geneous mixture and utilize direct-cylinder fuel injection which are characteristics of the compression-ignited diesel engine, but also employ spark ignition and sometimes throttling which are characteristics of the spark-ignited gasoline engine. Moreover, many stratified-charge engines exhibit multifuel capability.

These engine-type distinctions are blurred even more with methanol combustion. As discussed above, the two engine types have been designed and optimized for gasoline and diesel fuel com-bustion, respectively. Neither has been designed or optimized for methanol combustion. Not surprisingly, methanol's properties are such that the "ideal" methanol engine would utilize some of the characteristics of the spark-ignited gasoline engine as well as some of the characteristics of the compression-ignited diesel engine. The question then becomes how to classify the basic engine types in a discussion involving comparisons with methanol combustion. Of course, with methanol as a fuel the gasoline/diesel classification is meaningless. Because methanol's proper-ties make autoignition very difficult, it is not anticipated that any methanol engines would be able to rely solely on compression for ignition, so the spark-ignited/compression-ignited distinction is also not accurate. I have decided that for the purposes of this paper I will rely on a cylinder fuel-inducted/cylinder fuel-injected classification scheme. Basically, cylinder fuel-injected engines include all compression-ignited diesel engines (which, for methanol, will generally utilize some form of ignition assistance) as well as most stratified-charge engines, while cylinder fuel-inducted engines include all spark-ignited gasoline engines except for the stratified-charge engines. Since at this time there is little reported data involving methanol com-bustion in stratified-charge engines, this classification scheme will result in discussion which will parallel that which would have resulted using a gasoline/diesel breakdown. In the future, however, this cylinder fuel-inducted/cylinder fuel-injected classification scheme should be quite helpful.

It must be emphasized that the development of pure methanol vehicles is very much in a state of flux. Meaningful investiga-tions of pure methanol (or nearly pure methanol) in cylinder fuel-injected engines have only recently begun and much optimiza-tion work is still possible even for the more studied fuel-induc-ted engines. Also important, only this year will the first multi-vehicle pure methanol fleets go into operation which will provide important data in future years with respect to the possible deterioration of emissions and fuel efficiency in use. Thus, it can be expected that the data base on pure methanol vehicles will greatly expand in the next few years.

II. Properties of Methanol as a Vehicle Fuel

Methanol, whose chemical formula is CH_3OH, is the simplest alcohol. It is generally synthesized by the addition of two molecules of hydrogen to one molecule of carbon monoxide. Accordingly, its combustion properties are similar to these gases and distinct from the large hydrocarbon molecules which comprise gasoline and diesel fuels. The oxygen constitutes one-half of the methanol molecule's weight and forms a hydroxyl group making it strongly polar as compared with the nonpolar hydrocarbon fuels. These basic differences result in quite different vehicle fuel properties for methanol compared to gasoline and diesel fuels. The most important fuel combustion properties are summarized in Table 1.

From Table 1 it is apparent that methanol is quite distinct from gasoline and diesel fuels in many ways. The much lower energy density of methanol requires much larger fuel delivery and storage systems than those in use in current vehicles. Its much larger heat of vaporization means that methanol requires much greater amounts of heat to vaporize it. This has positive results, allowing increased cooling of intake air and engine parts (and thus greater efficiency), but can also cause mechanical problems and ignition delay. Methanol's lower vapor pressure (compared to gasoline) and lack of any low-boiling point components make it more difficult to cold-start. Methanol's higher octane number allows the use of greater compression ratios resulting in higher thermodynamic efficiencies, while its lower cetane number makes it more difficult to ignite in compression-ignition engines. Finally, methanol has a higher flame speed and correspondingly wider misfire limits. This allows methanol combustion to be leaner resulting in efficiency improvements. These distinct combustion properties are the primary determinants of the emissions and efficiency differences between methanol and petroleum (gasoline and diesel) fuels.

The following discussion will separate the use of neat methanol in cylinder fuel-inducted engines from use in cylinder fuel-injected engines. Because of its high octane and low cetane numbers, methanol has been studied in fuel-inducted engines much more so than in fuel-injected engines. This historical tendency is now changing somewhat as the emphasis on optimizing energy efficiency has encouraged researchers to experiment with the high compression, fuel-injected engine as a methanol powerplant and as new methods of facilitating such use become apparent. Much of the discussion below will report data from vehicles using both methanol and diesel fuels, with the former being used as the predominant fuel and the latter being used as a pilot fuel to initiate ignition.

III. Technical Feasibility

A. Cylinder Fuel-Inducted Engines

Methanol has been recognized as a fine fuel for fuel-inducted engines. Many of its most distinctive properties, such as its high heat of vaporization, high flame speed, and high octane number, are ideal for combustion in a fuel-inducted Otto-cycle engine. These properties strongly suggest the possibility of the development of a low emission, high energy economy and high performance power system with methanol usage in a fuel-inducted engine. In fact, conclusions from earlier experimental studies are now being coordinated and implemented into complete vehicle systems. It is now possible to build a fuel-inducted engine powered by methanol, and future work will likely involve optimization of emissions, fuel economy, and durability.

Of course, certain changes are necessary and/or desirable in changing from gasoline to methanol combustion in a fuel-inducted engine. These modifications revolve around three parameters -- maximizing engine thermal efficiency, minimizing cold-start difficulties, and resolving any corrosion or durability problems associated with methanol combustion.

The primary vehicle modification involved in increasing engine efficiency is an increase in the combustion chamber compression ratio. Such a change is easily accomplished at the manufacturing level. Most researchers have concluded that compression ratios in the 12:1 to 13:1 range are preferable for methanol combustion, as compared to the 8:1 to 9:1 ratios typical of current fuel-inducted engines operating on lower octane gasolines. Slight combustion chamber modifications will also likely be desirable to optimize efficiency at the higher compression ratios. Finally, because of methanol's much lower heating value and wide flammability limits, methanol engines would utilize a much different air/fuel ratio than current gasoline-inducted engines and thus relatively simple carburetion or fuel metering changes are necessary. The issue of energy efficiency will be quantitatively discussed later in this report.

Without special modifications, methanol-inducted engines experience cold-start difficulties at temperatures around 40°F.[5] Several possible solutions have been proposed and are being investigated. These include the blending of volatile, low boiling point components into the methanol (for example, isopentane), the use of electrical fuel preheaters, much better fuel nebulization, and even dissociation of methanol into gaseous carbon monoxide and hydrogen. Volkswagen was able to achieve good cold-starting capability at temperatures as low as −7°F with the addition of 5 to 10 percent of highly volatile substances to the methanol fuel.[5] Obviously, all of these would require some carburetion or fuel system modifications. Also suggested is the use of high-energy ignition systems to satisfy the demands of the higher compression ratios and to improve driveability after cold starting.[6]

Finally, there is the issue of durability of methanol engines. Because methanol contains no carbon-carbon bonds, there should be no soot deposit buildups in methanol engines. Volkswagen inspected the combustion chambers, valves, and pistons of a methanol-fueled Rabbit after 35,000 kilometers of operation and found them to be clean.[5] There is legitimate concern about methanol's corrosive nature. For example, methanol attacks the terne plate (lead-tin alloy coating) in fuel tanks, some alloys (especially zinc and aluminum) used in carburetor castings, and some nonmetallic parts. In addition, research at the Southwest Research Institute has indicated that pure methanol can cause up to 6 times more engine wear (cylinder bores, piston rings, engine bearings, etc.) during cold starts than unleaded gasoline, due primarily to the formic acid and formaldehyde produced during methanol combustion.[7] However, the same researchers have developed an additive which cuts methanol's engine wear rate in half, and it seems reasonable to expect that further materials and additives research will solve these corrosion and wear problems.

Manufacturers around the world have begun to produce or are developing the capability to produce fuel-inducted engines specifically designed for methanol. Volkswagen has had an active methanol development program since at least 1974. It is producing 100 pure methanol passenger cars for West Germany's Alcohol Fuels Project which will provide significant in-use data from 1980 through 1982. Volkswagen is also providing 15 to 20 methanol-inducted vehicles (Rabbits and pickup trucks utilizing manifold port injection upstream of the intake valve) to the State of California for the latter's three-year fleet test.[8] These vehicles are basically assembly-line vehicles and indicate that Volkswagen could likely mass produce methanol vehicles in the near future. Ford is supplying California with 40 methanol-powered Escorts which will have some modifications made off the assembly line.[8] Of course, Volkswagen, Ford, and many other world manufacturers have gained experience with designing and manufacturing alcohol vehicles as part of Brazil's ethanol program. By agreement between Brazil and the auto manufacturers, 200,000 neat ethanol cars were to be produced during 1980 and 900,000 by the end of 1982[9]. The experience of the manufacturers in mass producing ethanol vehicles will be of great value should they decide to mass produce methanol vehicles. This experience, along with the rather minor technical problems addressed above, indicates that there is very little question that methanol-inducted engines could be mass produced if that becomes desirable.

B.   Cylinder Fuel-Injected Engines

Cylinder fuel-injected engines can be divided into two
general types. The first type is what has come to be known as the
stratified-charge fuel-injected engine. This type of engine
shares some characteristics of both the spark-ignited gasoline
engine and the compression-ignited diesel engine. As such, some
have theorized that the stratified-charge fuel-injected engine
might be very well suited for methanol combustion. Although
several such designs are known, such as the Ford PROCO and the
White TCCS engines, there is no data base available for either of
these engines utilizing methanol as a fuel.

The second type of cylinder fuel-injected engine is the compression-ignited diesel engine. While methanol has always been
recognized as a fine fuel for spark-ignited fuel-inducted, Otto-
cycle engines, it has typically been characterized as a poor
fuel-injected, diesel-cycle fuel. The primary problem is methanol's very low cetane number, which makes autoignition due to
compression alone very difficult. This ignition problem in compression-ignited fuel-injected engines is much more serious than
in spark-ignited fuel-inducted engines, where serious problems
generally occur only during low ambient temperatures. Because of
this serious ignition difficulty, very little research has been
done concerning the use of pure methanol in cylinder fuel-injected
engines. But as fuel conservation has become of ever greater
importance, the possibility of combining an efficient fuel --
methanol -- with an efficient engine -- the high compression,
cylinder fuel-injected diesel cycle -- has received renewed attention.

Many possible solutions have been proposed for pure methanol's autoignition problems in the cylinder fuel-injected diesel-
cycle engine, making it, in effect, an ignition-assisted diesel
engine. These include intake air preheating, turbocharging,
higher compression ratios, glow plugs, and spark ignition. The
latter two methods have been receiving greater attention.
Researchers in Brazil have successfully operated a 3.9-liter,
4-cylinder engine with glow plugs to initiate surface ignition, a
design concept which takes advantage of the high detonation
("knocking") resistance and low surface (or "hot spot") pre-
ignition resistance of methanol.[10] While methanol requires
higher air-fuel mixture temperatures to self-ignite, the presence
of a hot surface has been shown to trigger pre-ignition of methanol to a greater extent than for other fuels; this is likely due
in part to the dissociation of methanol at high temperatures to
carbon monoxide and hydrogen, with the latter breaking down into
various radicals triggering pre-ignition.[11] While this surface
ignition phenomenon would be of some concern in a gasoline engine
because of the possibility of the center electrode of the spark
plug promoting pre-ignition in advance of the spark, it might be
advantageously utilized in a diesel engine to initiate combustion.

MAN of West Germany has recently modified a direct-injection diesel engine for pure methanol combustion. The two key aspects of the modification were the addition of spark ignition and the functional separation of fuel injection and mixture formation through the application of wall deposition of the methanol. MAN reports promising initial test results for the concept, including improved acceleration, better torque at full load, and no cold start difficulties. MAN has equipped an urban bus with one of their methanol-injected engines and it is being used as part of the German Alcohol Fuels Project.[12,13]

The use of cetane improving additives like amyl or hexyl nitrate or the use of dual-fuel injection systems (with a high cetane fuel used as pilot injection) have received considerable attention, though these methods cannot be said to utilize pure methanol. The German company KHD is providing 2 buses and 10 commercial vehicles utilizing the dual-fuel system for the German Alcohol Fuels Project.[12] Volvo has performed extensive testing investigating the possibilities for utilizing alcohol fuels in fuel-injected turbocharged diesel-cycle engines and has concluded that the most promising concept is the dual-fuel engine with two separate injection systems, one for small amounts of diesel pilot fuel and one for large amounts of methanol.[32] One can only speculate about the outcome of these projects, but it is clear that there are several possible solutions to methanol's auto-ignition difficulties in the diesel engine.

Other expected vehicle modifications would be similar to those discussed for fuel-inducted engines. Methanol's much lower heating value would require much larger injection pump flow rates. The fact that methanol combustion produces no soot would be beneficial, but the corrosion and wear problems mentioned in the previous section would likely apply to fuel-injected engines as well, and could be exasercbated by the fact that diesel-cycle engines typically have longer lives than Otto-cycle engines. One special problem for methanol combustion in diesel engines concerns its poor lubricity. Since diesel fuel is a good lubricant, it is used to lubricate parts of the injection pump. Pure methanol would likely cause accelerated wear of the injection pump components. Two possible solutions are the use of an oil lubricated pump (already available on the market) or the use of small amounts of castor oil blended directly into the methanol (though the side effects of the use of castor oil are unknown). Once again, this problem appears solvable in the near future.

One advantage of methanol-injection compared to diesel-injection is that the former appears capable of producing specific power outputs equal to, or greater than, those achieved by the latter. Apart from the possibility that methanol-injection might well result in higher thermodynamic efficiencies, there is also the fact that because of the very low (and possibly zero) smoke levels of pure methanol operation, higher fueling rates can be used without reaching the smoke limit.[14]

In conclusion, the development of pure methanol cylinder fuel-injected engines is not as far along as that of fuel-inducted engines. Research and development work should be expanded and expedited so that a reasoned decision can be made with respect to whether methanol should be encouraged for fuel-inducted or fuel-injected engines or both.

IV. Emissions

A. Cylinder Fuel-Inducted Engines

1. Organic (Unburned Fuel and Aldehyde Emissions)

Although gasoline-inducted engines emit measurable amounts of nonhydrocarbon organic compounds (for example, oxygenated species such as aldehydes and alcohols), the vast majority of organic emissions from gasoline-inducted engines are unburned fuel and the custom has been to focus attention on hydrocarbons as the most important class of organic emissions. Such a description would not be proper for emissions from methanol exhaust since oxygenated compounds predominate. Thus, the term "organic" emissions has been used to account for all of the unburned fuel, hydrocarbon, and aldehyde emissions from gasoline and methanol exhaust.

Most organic emissions in gasoline engine exhaust are the result of incomplete combustion. The primary cause of incomplete combustion is wall quenching, where the relatively cool combustion chamber wall prevents ideal propagation of the flame all the way to the wall. Other sources of incomplete combustion include poor condition of the ignition system such as fouled spark plugs, low charge temperature, too rich or too lean air-fuel ratios, and large exhaust residuals in the cylinder. One would expect these same phenomena to be the primary sources of incomplete combustion and organic emissions in methanol engine exhaust. Some of methanol's fuel properties such as its high octane number, high flame speed, and wider flammability limits (resulting, as we will show later, in a higher thermal efficiency for methanol as compared to gasoline) would tend to decrease incomplete combustion, while other properties such as its high heat of vaporization and low vapor pressure would tend to increase incomplete combustion. In terms of engine-out organic mass emissions it is not theoretically apparent whether methanol would be better or worse than gasoline. Empirical research must be relied upon to help us analyze these organic emissions questions.

Though several researchers have studied the issue of organic emissions from methanol exhaust as compared to gasoline exhaust, there has not been a consensus with respect to overall environmental impact of organic emissions. Even the structure of the discussion has varied among researchers. Some have compared total organic emissions, others have broken organic emissions down between unburned fuel (methanol in methanol exhaust, hydrocarbons in gasoline exhaust) and aldehydes. This latter breakdown makes the most sense, because aldehydes are generally only a relatively minor component of organic emissions on a mass basis, because aldehydes are of special concern from an air quality/public health basis, and because aldehydes are generally measured in a completely different way than are unburned fuel emissions.

Unburned fuel emissions from gasoline-inducted engines are typically measured by a flame ionization detector (FID), which measures the amount of ionizable carbon present in the exhaust sample, or, when condensation is a concern, by a heated FID (HFID). Because unburned methanol is water soluble, it is most appropriately measured by a HFID. Both the speed and magnitude of the HFID response are affected by the type of hydrocarbon in the sample. For unburned fuel measurement from gasoline-inducted engines, propane is used as the analyzer calibration gas. But the HFID detects the carbon atom in methanol with less sensitivity than it does the carbon atom in propane. Thus, two basic options are available for measuring unburned methanol emissions in a HFID. One, a specific concentration of methanol in a diluent gas can be used in calibration. Two, the analyzer can be calibrated with propane and corrected for the relative response to methanol as compared to propane. The relative response to methanol as compared to propane can be experimentally determined, and has been found to range from 0.73 to 0.85.[15,16,17,18] Obviously, unburned methanol emissions data from a HFID calibrated with propane must be corrected in order to be meaningful.

A second issue with respect to unburned methanol emissions concerns its oxygen component. The unburned fuel emissions from gasoline-inducted engines are composed almost exclusively of carbon and hydrogen, and thus the hydrocarbon mass can be determined by simply using the H/C ratio of the gasoline. Methanol, however, is half oxygen by weight and the question arises as to whether the emissions measurements should be reported as total grams per mile unburned methanol (which would include the oxygen component) or grams per mile ionizable carbon or grams per mile ionizable carbon plus associated hydrogen (both of which would not include the oxygen component). Researchers have reported results in all of these ways, and it is important to identify the methodology used in reporting such results since the inclusion of the oxygen component of unburned methanol will produce twice the mass measurement compared to excluding the oxygen component.

The situation is somewhat more straightforward with respect to aldehyde mass emissions measurement and reporting. Determination of total aldehydes is nearly universally performed by using the 3-methyl-2-benzothiazolone hydrazone hydrochloride (MBTH) technique. Measurements of aldehyde emissions from both gasoline and methanol-fueled vehicles are generally reported as formaldehyde, which is the predominant aldehyde in both types of exhausts.[19]

Keeping in mind the above remarks, the following results have been reported in the literature for unburned fuel and aldehyde emissions from methanol-inducted and gasoline-inducted engines. Ingamells and Lindquist modified a 1971 compact car and found unburned fuel emissions to be twice as high with methanol without a catalytic converter but approximately equal with a converter (total methanol mass basis); aldehyde emissions were approximately equal without the converter.[1] Hilden and Parks used a single-cylinder engine without catalytic reduction but with "standard" and "improved" vaporization. With standard vaporization, unburned fuel emissions were four times greater with methanol but with improved vaporization the unburned fuel emissions were approximately equal (total methanol mass basis). Aldehyde emissions were 10 times and 3 to 4 times greater with methanol for standard and improved vaporization, respectively.[15] Menrad, Lee, and Bernhardt modified a VW Rabbit without a catalytic converter. They found unburned fuel emissions to be 4 times lower with methanol (on a total methanol mass basis) and aldehyde emissions to be somewhat higher.[17] Brinkman modified a 1975 car utilizing manifold port injection upstream of the intake valve and tested it with and without a catalytic converter. Engine-out unburned fuel emissions were 3.5 times greater and tailpipe (with catalyst) unburned fuel emissions were 5 times greater with methanol (total methanol mass basis) under near-stoichiometric conditions.[20] Pischinger and Kramer performed a series of tests on a single-cylinder engine without an oxidation catalyst and found aldehyde emissions to generally be 2 to 3 times greater with methanol.[21] Bechtold and Pullman tested a 1976 full-size Dodge vehicle at two air/fuel ratios (stoichiometric and 20 percent lean) and two compression ratios (8.5:1 and 13:1). All their unburned fuel data were reported as ionizable carbon only. At the standard (i.e., gasoline) compression ratio and stoichiometry, unburned fuel emissions were twice as great with methanol without the oxidation catalyst but only one-half as much with the catalyst. Under lean operation the unburned fuel emissions with methanol were 40 percent greater without the catalyst and 20 percent less with the catalyst. Under the higher compression ratio only the catalyst condition was tested. Unburned fuel emissions with methanol were approximately one-half as great as those with gasoline under both stoichiometric and lean conditions. The same researchers also tested three 1978 Ford Pintos equipped with three-way-catalysts at the standard 8.5:1 compression ratio and stoichiometry. Unburned fuel emissons were about half for methanol compared to gasoline. Aldehydes were 6 times greater from methanol.[16] Finally, Baisley and Edwards also tested some 1978 Pintos with three-way-catalysts. Unburned fuel emissions with methanol were one-half of those with gasoline (on an ionizable carbon basis) while aldehydes were 3 times greater with methanol.[19]

What tentative conclusions can be drawn from the above results? The first five studies all reported unburned methanol on a mass basis. Except for the Rabbit data, all the results showed unburned methanol emissions to be equal to or up to 5 times greater than unburned gasoline emissions. The final two studies reported unburned fuel emissions on the basis of ionizable carbon. Per carbon atom, the actual mass of unburned methanol is 2.3 times that of gasoline (methanol's molecular weight of 32 divided by a typical weight of 13.85 for gasoline). Thus, one would expect the final two sets of data to be more promising for methanol, and they are, with the catalyst data consistently less for methanol than for gasoline. If we were to multiply the final two sets of data by 2.3, however, the methanol data would be equal to or somewhat greater than the gasoline data and thus would be in fair agreement with the earlier studies. The aldehyde data clearly indicate that methanol-fueled engines emit greater amounts of aldehydes, generally on the order of 2 to 6 times as many as gasoline-fueled vehicles.

Besides the conflicting test results and reporting methodologies, other factors also make a comparison of the organic emissions from gasoline and methanol exhausts very difficult. Many of the early comparative studies used single-cylinder engines or vehicles which did not utilize any type of exhaust aftertreatment. It has been demonstrated that catalytic converters are very efficient at reducing methanol and aldehyde emissions.[20,21,22] Even more importantly, it must be emphasized that the past comparisons between methanol-inducted and gasoline-inducted single-cylinder engines and vehicles have clearly by necessity been somewhat biased in favor of the gasoline-fueled vehicles. After all, the study of organic (hydrocarbon) emissions from gasoline-inducted vehicles has been a central concern for automotive engineers for over a decade and engine design, fuel system delivery design, and converter technology have all been optimized for low organic emissions from gasoline-fueled engines. Certainly, organic emissions from methanol combustion, which involve completely different species, have not been subjected to the same degree of analysis or controls, and it seems likely that a reasonable amount of progress could be achieved if the necessary resources were expended. A few studies have appeared which justify such optimism. For example, it has been demonstrated that part of the reason for discrepancies in the measurements of unburned fuel emissions in methanol exhaust is due to the preparation of the air/fuel mixture; methanol is much more difficult to vaporize than gasoline and those researchers who have made extra efforts to improve methanol vaporization have generally reported lower relative emissions of unburned methanol.[15] Studies of aldehyde formation in methanol engines should facilitate the development of designs to lower aldehyde emissions.[11,23]

The above discussion indicates that it is not now possible to determine whether organic emissions, on a mass basis, will be greater or less for a methanol-inducted engine relative to a gasoline-inducted engine. It must be remembered, however, that the most serious environmental problem associated with organic emissions in general is their role as oxidant precursors in urban atmospheres. As such, the relative <u>masses</u> of organic emissions in gasoline and methanol exhausts are <u>not as</u> important as the relative <u>reactivities</u> of the organic emissions. Though aldehydes (and particularly formaldehyde), which are generally emitted in greater amounts by methanol-inducted engines, are known to be reactive, methanol combustion produces almost no alkenes, aromatics, or non-methane alkanes which are the most reactive components of gasoline exhaust. Thus, it is not immediately clear whether methanol exhaust would be more or less reactive than gasoline exhaust.

Recently published research by Bechtold and Pullman has shed additional light on the relative reactivities of methanol and gasoline exhausts.[16] They performed two different types of smog chamber experiments to determine relative gasoline and methanol exhaust reactivities, in both cases using surrogate organic compounds to represent the organic compounds in the actual exhausts. In the first set of experiments, the initial NOx concentration in the smog chamber was held constant at 0.40 parts per million, regardless of the NOx concentration in the vehicle exhaust. The various measures of reactivity, such as the maximum ozone and nitrogen dioxide concentrations and the time it takes to reach them, were comparable for gasoline and methanol exhausts for all vehicles and operating conditions tested. In the second set of experiments, the initial NOx concentrations in the smog chamber were varied in proportion to the NOx emissions concentrations in the gasoline-fueled and methanol-fueled vehicles' exhausts. Under stoichiometric conditions, the methanol exhaust was less reactive in terms of <u>every</u> parameter examined. At lean engine operation, the results were mixed with methanol exhaust yielding the higher maximum ozone concentration but gasoline exhaust yielding the higher nitrogen dioxide concentration. Of considerable relevance was the finding that the maximum formaldehyde concentrations in many of the smog chamber tests with gasoline exhaust exceeded those from the tests with methanol exhaust. Even though the initial formaldehyde concentrations were much greater in the methanol exhaust, much more formaldehyde was formed (probably from alkene oxidation) during the photochemical process from the gasoline exhaust. This is a very important consideration since formaldehyde is a suspected carcinogen.

In addition, it must be noted that the use of neat methanol fuel is expected to greatly reduce evaporative organic emissions. As noted above, the vapor pressure of methanol is considerably lower than that of gasoline, and for pure fuels vapor pressure is a good indicator of evaporative emissions. This property is very important since as exhaust organic emissions levels have been lowered the evaporative component has become more important. For example, EPA's emission factors indicate that by the mid-1980's evaporative emissions will account for as much as one-fifth of all zero-mile gasoline-powered vehicle organic emissions, though the relative percentage from the evaporative component lessens with vehicle age. Since evaporative emissions contain no methane component, they are of considerable interest with respect to reactivity. Thus, less evaporative emissions from methanol will also decrease the reactivities of urban atmospheres.

2.   Carbon Monoxide Emissions

Very little discussion of the effect of methanol's usage in fuel-inducted engines on carbon monoxide levels is necessary. CO levels are primarily a function of the air/fuel ratio, with more CO formed as the mixture becomes richer. Practically all of the published studies agree that at stoichiometric air/fuel conditions, CO levels in methanol exhaust are very similar to those in gasoline exhaust.[1,15,17,20] Because methanol can be operated at leaner air/fuel ratios, there is a good possibility of even lower CO levels. One study reported CO emissions from a methanol-fueled vehicle operating 14 percent lean to be 30 percent less than the same vehicle operating at 5 percent lean (the maximum leanness for good driveability) on gasoline.[1] Another study showed engine CO emissions from a methanol-fueled vehicle to drop from 23 grams per mile (gpm) at 4 percent lean to 10 gpm at 17 percent lean to 7 gpm at 38 percent lean. Similarly, tailpipe CO emissions (including aftertreatment) were 5.5 gpm, 3.9 gpm, and 1.6 gpm, respectively.[20]

3.   NOx Emissions

Nitric oxide is formed from the reaction of atomic oxygen or nitrogen with molecules of nitrogen or oxygen. The reactions are very slow, with half-lives on the same order as the expansion stroke in an engine. The formation of NO is thus primarily governed by the kinetics rather than the equilibrium considerations, and as a result, has a very strong exponential temperature dependence.[4] As methanol combusts at a lower flame temperature compared to gasoline, and because methanol can operate at leaner air/fuel ratios as well (also lowering peak temperatures), NOx emissions are inherently lower in a methanol-fueled engine. In fact, this characteristic of methanol combustion provided some of the impetus for early methanol studies.

A search of the literature shows a general consensus that methanol-inducted engines produce approximately one-half of the NOx emissions of gasoline-inducted engines at similar operating conditions, with individual studies showing reductions of from 30 percent to 65 percent.[1,20,21,24,25] One of the major engine design changes expected with methanol-inducted engines is the use of higher compression ratios to increase engine effficiency. Experiments have confirmed the theoretical expectation that higher compression ratios, with no other design changes, increase NOx emissions considerably due to the higher combustion temperatures.[17,26] But, due to the high compression ratio, less spark timing advance is needed. Retarding spark timing is known to reduce both NOx emissions and engine efficiency. Fortunately, it has been shown that the combination of a much larger compression ratio with a few degrees of spark timing retard can both increase thermal efficiency and decrease NOx emissions.[26] Thus, the use of methanol might make it possible for vehicles to meet the current 1.0 gpm NOx standard without the need for a NOx-reducing catalyst.

The lower NOx emissions from methanol-induced vehicles would have two major beneficial environmental impacts. First, as discussed in the section on organic emissions, the lower NOx emissions would decrease the reactivity of methanol exhaust in urban atmospheres. Second, lower NOx vehicle emissions would help alleviate the serious acid rain problems which are of paramount concern in certain areas of the country.

4. Sulfur Emissions

It is anticipated that the sulfur levels in methanol fuel will be zero or near zero because of requirements in the methanol production synthesis process. Thus, there will be no possibility of any consequential amounts of sulfur-containing pollutants. This will again be an advantage compared to gasoline-fueled vehicles which, because of the catalyst material in the converter and small amounts of sulfur in the fuel, emit small amounts of sulfuric acid mist.

B. Cylinder Fuel-Injected Engines

As stated above, cylinder fuel-injected engines include both the spark-ignited stratified-charge engine and the compression-ignited diesel engine. Although the former is thought to be a promising powerplant for methanol-injection, there is not much of a data base in the literature on the emissions or fuel efficiency of methanol-injected stratified-charge engines. Therefore, the discussions of the emissions and fuel efficiencies of methanol-injected engines will necessarily concentrate on diesel-cycle engines, generally with some sort of ignition assistance.

1. Particulate Emissions

From a welfare standpoint, diesel particulate has long been considered both an aesthetic problem (as "smoke," the visible component of particulate, which does not always correlate with particulate mass emissions) and as a contributor to urban visibility problems. It has also been well established that particulate matter can increase the prevalence of chronic respiratory disease in healthy adults and the aggravation of bronchitis, emphysema, and asthma in susceptible persons. In the last few years, diesel particulate has become of much more concern, due to its small size, its greater relative impact on air quality where people live and work (compared to other large sources of particulate emissions), and the finding that its extractable organic fraction is mutagenic in short-term bioassays.[27] EPA, other government agencies, and private industry are spending millions of dollars to determine the carcinogenic risk of diesel particulate to public health. Even absent an absolute finding on the cancer issue, particulate emissions have become of such concern that EPA has promulgated standards for diesel passenger cars and light trucks and proposed standards for heavy diesel trucks.[28,29]

Diesel particulate consists of solid carbonaceous particles (soot) and liquid aerosols. The former are generally formed when fuel-rich mixture pockets burn and form solid particulate. This solid particulate can then serve as a nuclei for more harmful organic species to adsorb onto and as a "vehicle" for such compounds to reach (and possibly lodge in) the lung's bronchial region. Although large reductions in engine-out particulate have been reported, particulate matter seems to be an inherent pollutant in diesel-injected compression-ignition engines.

Methanol has no carbon-carbon bonds and has not been observed to form carbonaceous particles.[14] In addition, methanol does not contain inorganic materials like sulfur or lead which can also be sources of solid particulate. Accordingly, with pure methanol there would be no nuclei for liquid aerosols to adsorb onto and total particulate emissions would be expected to be zero.[30] Unfortunately, there appear to be no studies which have measured particulate emissions from diesel-injected engines burning neat methanol. There is a small data base in the literature on the effect of methanol injection on smoke levels in diesel-cycle engines. Smoke levels are a measure of the visible fraction of particulate matter. As such, smoke levels do not correlate perfectly with particulate emission levels but are generally directionally consistent. The MAN spark-ignited pure methanol-injected engine reportedly exhibited no exhaust discoloration whatsoever in initial tests under full load conditions. A similar MAN compression-ignited diesel-injected engine exhibited smoke levels of between 1 and 3 Bosch smoke units over the same full load conditions.[13] Several studies have reported lower smoke levels for dual-fuel engines using diesel pilot fuel and methanol as the primary combustion fuel, both in single-cylinder tests and in tests of the Volvo dual-fuel engine.[10,31,32] Recently EPA confirmed these results for the Volvo dual-fuel engine, finding that smoke levels for the dual-fuel engine when using methanol as the primary fuel were consistently lower than smoke levels for the baseline diesel-injected engine, especially under transient and power curve testing. Particulate emission levels were approximately one-half as high with the methanol/diesel dual-fuel Volvo engine compared to the baseline diesel-injected engine.[36] Although the 50 percent particulate reduction is significant, particulate emissions were not zero. It must be noted that the Volvo dual-fuel engine utilized approximately 20 percent diesel fuel by weight and it seems likely that it was this diesel combustion that produced the particulate emissions. There seems to be very little question that neat methanol combustion in cylinder fuel-injected engines would result in very low (and possibly zero) particulate emissions, which would provide a very important environmental advantage compared to diesel fuel combustion.

2. Organic (Unburned Fuel and Aldehyde) Emissions

There is very little data on the relative organic emission levels of fuel-injected engines using methanol and diesel fuels, and what data there are generally involve dual-fuel engines which combust meaningful amounts of diesel fuel. Such engines would not be expected to have the same organic emissions as pure methanol-injected engines. One study using methanol with diesel pilot fuel in a single-cylinder engine reported considerably higher organic emissions while another study under similar conditions reported equal or somewhat lower organic emissions.[33,31] Volvo reported that in very limited testing their dual-fuel-injected, turbocharged engine emitted equal or slightly less organic emissions with methanol depending on the load range.[32] Recent EPA testing of the Volvo dual-fuel engine showed higher organic emissions compared to the baseline diesel-injected engine.[36] In an independent review of the literature, Ricardo recently concluded that alcohol-injected engines would likely produce more organic emissions than diesel-injected engines, especially at lower loads.[14] Conclusions with respect to this issue are difficult because of the scarce data base for pure methanol-injected combustion (compared to dual-fuel injection) as well as confusion over how to measure and report organic emission levels (see the discussion under fuel-inducted engines). Much more work is necessary with respect to the measurement and characterization of organic emissions from methanol-injected engines.

There is no data base with respect to aldehyde emission levels from pure methanol-injected engines. The only data available involved dual-fuel engines. One researcher reported less aldehydes with a dual-fuel engine than with pure diesel fuel combustion.[31] EPA testing of the Volvo dual-fuel engine resulted in much higher aldehyde emissions--4.5 times more aldehydes for the methanol/diesel dual-fuel engine than for the baseline diesel-injected engine during steady-state testing and 18 times more aldehydes during transient testing.[36] Aldehyde emissions are a serious concern from methanol-injected engines, particularly since formaldehyde, the principal aldehyde from methanol combustion, has been shown to be carcinogenic. One possible solution for unburned methanol and aldehydes is aftertreatment, as catalytic converters have been found to be effective at oxidizing these compounds. The two reasons why it has been difficult to design an effective diesel catalytic converter are the lower diesel exhaust gas temperatures and the high particulate emission rates (which tend to clog up the converter). Methanol usage would exascerbate the first problem as it appears to produce even

lower exhaust gas temperatures (which is positive from an efficiency standpoint) but methanol's particulate-free combustion
would remove the second obstacle to diesel converter development.[10] MAN reports promising results with catalytic aftertreatment on their spark-ignited, methanol-injected bus
engine.[13] EPA tested the Volvo dual-fuel engine with an oxidation catalyst which was not optimized for the Volvo engine. It
lowered hydrocarbon emissions by approximately 90 percent and
unburned methanol emissions by from 57 to 82 percent, but actually
increased aldehyde emissions somewhat.[36] Catalyst development
for unburned methanol and aldehyde emissions reduction is an area
where improvements can be expected.

Of course, as discussed in a previous section, it is not the
mass of organic emissions but rather the emissions' reactivity
that is of the greatest importance. No diesel-injected engine
organics versus methanol-injected engine organics smog chamber
studies have been reported. Given that diesel exhaust organics
are generally thought to be more reactive than gasoline exhaust
organics (especially for gasoline engines with catalytic converters where a significant portion of the organics is nonreactive
methane) and that we previously concluded that methanol exhaust
organics (at least in fuel-inducted engines) would likely be less
reactive than gasoline exhaust organics, it would appear plausible
that methanol exhaust organics may well be less reactive than
diesel exhaust organics.

Finally, as was discussed in the previous section, it is
thought that methanol will avoid the particulate/cancer problems
of the diesel-injected engine. One reason is that there are not
the solid particulate nuclei for organics to adsorb onto and which
can carry the organics deep into the lung. Also critical is that
methanol exhaust will not contain significant amounts of the
long-chain and multi-ring hydrocarbons which are of the greatest
public health concern, although recent studies on formaldehyde
would certainly indicate that the carcinogenic risk from methanol
exhaust is not zero.

3.   Carbon Monoxide Emissions

Again the data is very sketchy but theoretically one would
expect methanol-injected engines to produce similar levels of CO
as diesel-injected engines.[30] Two different single-cylinder,
dual-fuel studies did show comparable CO emissions.[31,33] EPA
found that the Volvo dual-fuel engine produced 2 to 3 times more
CO than its diesel-injected counterpart.[36] The unthrottled
fuel-injected engine's inherent lean combustion combined with
methanol's lean combustion and good efficiency ensure that CO
levels would be reasonably low on a pure methanol-injected engine.

4.   NOx Emissions

As with fuel-inducted engines, methanol's lower flame temperature should facilitate lower NOx emission levels from methanol-injected engines than from diesel-injected engines. Again, the single-cylinder, dual-fuel tests support this hypothesis, with one of the tests reporting NOx levels one-half as high as those from pure diesel operation.[31,33] EPA testing of the Volvo dual-fuel engine produced NOx reductions of from 35 to 56 percent as compared to the diesel-injected baseline engine.[36] MAN reports that their spark-ignited methanol-injected bus engine emitted 3.0 grams of NOx per horsepower-hour over the 13-mode test, a level approximately one-half of the best NOx levels of current diesel-injected engines. Methanol combustion would not only help alleviate acid rain and ambient NO_2 problems, but would also provide a long-term solution to the problem of reducing NOx levels from heavy-duty diesel engines which are currently unable to meet the Clean Air Act mandate for NOx emissions. As with fuel-inducted engines, lower NOx emissions would be one of the most important environmental advantages of methanol combustion in fuel-injected engines.

5.   Sulfur Emissions

Diesel fuel contains from 0.1 to 0.5 percent sulfur. The major sulfur product in diesel exhaust is sulfur dioxide which can be converted to sulfuric acid in the atmosphere. Since methanol would not contain any sulfur because of production requirements, it would not produce any sulfur pollutants. This would again reduce the acid rain burden slightly.

V.   Fuel Efficiency

A.   Cylinder Fuel-Inducted Engines

As shown in a previous section, methanol has a very low heating value, approximately one-half that of gasoline on a volumetric basis. But it is energy (such as Btu's) which is to be conserved, not volume of fuel, and so to be meaningful methanol and gasoline should be compared not on a mpg basis, but rather on an energy efficiency basis (for example, miles per million Btu). This discussion will limit itself to comparisons on an energy efficiency basis. In addition, the following efficiency comparisons will be on a relative basis and not on an absolute basis. In other words, if engine A is 10 percent more efficient than engine B that does not mean that engine A has a thermodynamic efficiency which is 10 percentage points greater than engine B, rather it means that engine A is, say, 33 percent efficient compared to engine B's 30 percent efficiency.

There is general agreement among researchers that methanol is a more energy efficient vehicle fuel than gasoline. There are theoretical reasons why this is so. Methanol's lower flame temperature reduces the amount of heat transfer from the combustion chamber to the vehicle coolant system. Its high heat of vaporization acts as an internal coolant and reduces the mixture temperature during the compression stroke. These characteristics increase methanol's thermodynamic efficiency, and are realized in experiments without having to make any major design changes from current vehicles. Studies have shown these inherent properties of methanol to increase the relative energy efficiency of a fuel-inducted passenger vehicle by from 3 to 10 percent with a middle range of about 5 percent.[17,20,25]

Other properties of neat methanol combustion allow even greater efficiency improvements. Its wider flammability limits and higher flame speeds relative to gasoline allow methanol to be combusted at leaner conditions while still providing good engine performance. This lean burning capability allows more complete combustion and improves energy efficiency. Early testing on a single-cylinder fuel-inducted engine yielded estimated energy efficiency improvements of 10 percent due to leaning of the methanol mixture as compared to gasoline tests; subsequent vehicle testing has shown relative efficiency improvements of lean methanol combustion of 6 to 8 percent, and 14 percent, respectively.[34,1,20] Given these results, it would seem that methanol's lean burning capability may yield as much as a 10 percent relative efficiency improvement.

Methanol's higher octane number allows the usage of higher compression ratios with correspondingly higher thermal efficiencies. Of course, there is a practical limit to compression ratio increases due to increased friction losses. Early single-cylinder testing estimated the relative thermal energy efficiency improvements of the higher compression ratios to be in the range of 16 to 20 percent.[26,34] Unfortunately, little vehicle data exists to confirm these figures, but it must be expected that improvements of up to 10 percent are likely.

Adding up the possible improvements indicates that methanol-inducted engines may well be as much as 25 percent more energy efficient than their gasoline counterparts. Volkswagen has reported energy efficiency improvements of approximately 15 percent for its mid-1970's methanol vehicles, with a corresponding power output increase of approximately 20 percent.[35] While it is true that emissions concerns may force some tradeoffs (the NOx/efficiency tradeoff has already been discussed) in terms of efficiency, it is also true that so far methanol energy efficiency data have been obtained using vehicles which were designed and optimized for gasoline-fueling and not for methanol combustion. As with emissions, time and resources will allow much methanol-specific optimization which should improve the energy efficiency of methanol-inducted engines even more.

B. Cylinder Fuel-Injected Engines

It has already been stated that there are several reasons why methanol is much more efficient than gasoline in fuel-inducted engines; the improvement has been estimated to be as much as 25 percent on an energy basis which is similar to the efficiency advantage often quoted for current diesel-fueled vehicles compared to current gasoline-fueled vehicles. Some of those characteristics which make methanol efficient in the fuel-inducted engine, such as its low flame temperature and low exhaust gas temperature, also are advantageous in the high compression, fuel-injected engine. Some of its other properties are not of much help, however, such as its high heat of vaporization (which simply makes it that much more difficult to ignite), lean combustion (which is inherent in diesel-cycle operation anyway) and high octane number.

Again, there is a dearth of information on pure methanol combustion in high compression, fuel-injected engines. One set of data involving pure methanol (with 1 to 2 percent castor oil for lubricity) utilized a 3.9-liter, 4-cylinder engine with glow plugs to initiate surface ignition. Steady-state tests with this engine showed significantly higher brake thermal efficiencies for methanol compared to diesel fuel above 30 percent load, ranging as high as 22 percent greater, while diesel fuel was more efficient at lower loads.[10] A second set of data involving pure methanol involves the MAN spark-ignited methanol-injected concept. Initially a non-commercial air-cooled 4-cylinder engine was modified and installed in a small 2-ton cross-country vehicle; methanol operation resulted in 12 percent better fuel economy than the diesel counterpart (test procedures unknown). More recently, in a simulation of urban traffic conditions, the MAN bus engine described earlier gave 5 percent better fuel economy than the corresponding diesel-injected engine.[13] One other single-cylinder, dual-fuel study reported slightly higher efficiency for methanol, while two other dual-fuel studies, one with a single-cylinder engine and the other the Volvo dual-fuel turbocharged engine, also showed methanol to be somewhat more efficient at higher loads but similar to diesel fuel at lower loads. [31,32,33] EPA found the Volvo dual-fuel engine to be approximately 5 percent less energy efficient than the diesel-injected baseline engine over the new transient test procedure, though most and probably all of the difference can be attributed to the fact that the injection timing of the dual-fuel engine was retarded five degrees from the diesel-injected baseline engine.[36]

It cannot be overstated that much work needs to be done in the area of methanol use in cylinder fuel-injected engines. The primary problem has been the initiation of combustion, and researchers continue to examine several solutions including pilot fuels (usually diesel fuel), glow plugs, spark ignition, cetane-improving additives, etc. Once a preferred design can be identified, serious optimization work can begin. Based on the early engine results reported above and the huge opportunity for basic improvements in this area, it seems likely that, should methanol prove feasible in high compression, fuel-injected engines, it will actually be a slightly more energy efficient fuel. Even if it should only match diesel fuel in energy efficiency, it would provide many environmental benefits (primarily particulate and NOx emissions reductions) as compared to diesel fuel.

VI. Conclusions

A.   Cylinder Fuel-Inducted Engines

There is little question about the technical feasibility of methanol combustion in fuel-inducted engines and several manufacturers (most notably Ford and Volkswagen) are now involved in the development of prototype and experimental fleet vehicles. Methanol use in fuel-inducted engines would reduce NOx emissions by approximately one-half, would result in similar or somewhat lower CO emissions, and would reduce sulfur emissions to zero. At this time, the data suggest that methanol combustion would reduce the total reactivities of the organic components of fuel-inducted engine exhaust, but this thesis is preliminary and more research must be undertaken. Particular emphasis must be placed on the control of formaldehyde emissions which are very reactive and likely carcinogenic. Methanol-inducted engines would definitely be more energy efficient than their gasoline-inducted counterparts, possibly by as much as 25 percent. Further research and optimization may allow additional improvements, but even absent further progress it now appears that methanol-inducted engines will be preferable to gasoline-inducted engines both in terms of energy efficiency and environmental pollution.

B.   Cylinder Fuel-Injected Engines

Methanol has always been considered a poor compression-ignition, fuel-injected engine fuel because of its poor auto-ignition. Thus, while greater emphasis has recently been placed on methanol combustion in fuel-injected engines, this development is not as far along as that with fuel-inducted engines and any conclusions are much more tentative. Methanol use in fuel-injected engines would likely result in zero or near-zero particulate emissions, considerably lower NOx emissions, zero sulfur emissions, and approximately equal CO emissions. Again, the data base is very sketchy with respect to organic emissions. On a mass basis, methanol-injected engines may produce greater amounts of organic emissions than diesel-injected engines. But it is impossible at this time to predict the effect of pure methanol-injection on the reactivity of fuel-injected engine exhaust. Given that current diesel-injected engine exhaust organics are generally considered more reactive than current gasoline-inducted engine (with catalytic converter) exhaust organics and that we have previously concluded that methanol exhaust organics (at least in fuel-inducted engines) would likely be less reactive than gasoline exhaust organics, it appears possible that methanol exhaust might well be less reactive than diesel exhaust. Research must be expedited in this area, especially with respect to the characterization and control of formaldehyde emissions. Methanol-injected engines would likely result in similar or somewhat greater energy efficiencies than diesel-injected engines, though research could produce greater improvements. The primary benefits of methanol usage in fuel-injected engines would be the significant particulate and NOx emission reductions.

References

1. "Methanol as a Motor Fuel or a Gasoline Blending Component," J. C. Ingamells and R. H. Lindquest, SAE Paper No. 750123.

2. "The Utilization of Alternative Fuels in a Diesel Engine Using Different Methods," E. Holmer, P. S. Berg, and B. I. Bertilsson, SAE Paper No. 800544.

3. "Toxicological Aspects of Alcohol Fuel Utilization," Andrew J. Moriarity, International Symposium on Alcohol Fuel Technology, Methanol, and Ethanol, November 21-23, 1977, CONF-771175.

4. Methanol Technology and Application in Motor Fuels, Edited by J. K. Paul, Noyes Data Corporation, 1978, pp. 39-81 and 326-374.

5. "Methanol Fuels in Automobiles--Experiences at Volkswagenwerk AG and Conclusions for Europe," Dr. Ing. W. Bernhardt, Volkswagenwerk AG, Wolfsburg, Germany.

6. "The Part of Volkswagenwerk AG in the German Program for Research on Alcohol Fuels," Holger Menrad, Fifth International Symposium on Automotive Propulsion Systems, April 14-18, 1980, DOE CONF-800419.

7. Synfuels Newsletter, December 12, 1980.

8. "Senate Bill 620: Alcohol Fuels Program," Staff Report, California Energy Commission, January 1981.

9. "Alcohol Cars in Brazil's Future: A Technological Forecast," Robert S. Goodrich, Paper C-25, Fourth International Symposium on Alcohol Fuels Technology, October 5-8, 1980.

10. "Use of Glow-Plugs in Order to Obtain Multifuel Capability of Diesel Engines," Instituto Maua de Tecnologia, Fourth International Symposium on Alcohol Fuels Technology, Brazil, October 5-8, 1980.

11. "Thermokinetic Modeling of Methanol Combustion Phenomena with Application to Spark Ignition Engines," L. H. Browning and R. K. Pefley, Paper I-16, Third International Symposium on Alcohol Fuels Technology, May 29-31, 1979, Published by DOE in April 1980.

12. "Objectives and First Results of the German Federal Alcohol Fuels Project," H. Quadflieg, T. U. V. Rheinland, and J. Bandel, Fourth International Symposium on Alcohol Fuels Technology, Brazil, October 5-8, 1980.

13.   "Results of MAN-FM Diesel Engines Operating on Straight Alcohol Fuels," A. Neitz and F. Chmela, Fourth International Symposium on Alcohol Fuels Technology, Brazil, October 5-8, 1980.

14.   "The Utilization of Alcohol in Light-Duty Diesel Engines," Ricardo Consulting Engineers, EPA-460/3-81-010, May 28, 1981.

15.   "A Single-Cylinder Engine Study of Methanol Fuel - Emphasis on Organic Emissions," David L. Hilden and Fred B. Parks, SAE Paper No. 760378.

16.   "Driving Cycle Economy, Emissions, and Photochemical Reactivity Using Alcohol Fuels and Gasoline," Richard Bechtold and J. Barrett Pullman, SAE Paper No. 800260.

17.   "Development of a Pure Methanol Fuel Car," Holger Menrad, Wenpo Lee, and Winfried Bernhardt, SAE Paper No. 770790.

18.   "Engine Performance and Exhaust Emissions: Methanol Versus Isooctane," G. D. Ebersole and F. S. Manning, SAE Paper No. 720692.

19.   "Emission and Wear Characteristics of an Alcohol Fueled Fleet Using Feedback Carburetion and Three-Way Catalysts," W. H. Baisley and C. F. Edwards, Fourth International Symposium on Alcohol Fuels Technology, Brazil, October 5-8, 1980.

20.   "Vehicle Evaluation of Neat Methanol - Compromises Among Exhaust Emissions, Fuel Economy and Driveability," Norman D. Brinkman, Energy Research, Vol. 3, pp. 243-274, 1979.

21.   "The Influence of Engine Parameters on the Aldehyde Emissions of a Methanol Operated Four-Stroke Otto Cycle Engine," Franz F. Pischinger and Klaus Kramer, Paper II-25, Third International Symposium on Alcohol Fuels Technology, May 29-31, 1979, Published by DOE in April 1980.

22.   "Alcohol Engine Emissions - Emphasis on Unregulated Compounds," M. Matsuno et al., Paper III-64, Third International Symposium on Alcohol Fuels Technology, May 29-31, 1979, Published by DOE in April 1980.

23.   "Formaldehyde Emissions From a Spark Ignition Engine Using Methanol," Kenichi Ito and Toshiaki Yano, Paper III-66, Third International Symposium on Alcohol Fuels Technology, May 29-31, 1979, Published by DOE in April 1980.

24.   "Research and Development - Alcohol Fuel Usage in Automobiles," University of Santa Clara, DOE Automotive Technology Development Contractor Coordination Meeting, November 13, 1980.

25. "A Motor Vehicle Powerplant for Ethanol and Methanol Operation," H. Menrad, Paper II-26, Third International Symposium on Alcohol Fuels Technology, May 29-31, 1979, Published by DOE in April 1980.

26. "Effect of Compression Ratio on Exhaust Emissions and Performance of a Methanol-Fueled Single-Cylinder Engine," Norman D. Brinkman, SAE Paper No. 770791.

27. "Application of Bioassay to the Characterization of Diesel Particulate Emissions," Huisingh, J., et al., Presented at the Symposium on Application of Short-Term Bioassays in the Fractionation and Analysis of Complex Environmental Mixtures," Williamsburg, Virginia, February 21-23, 1978.

28. Federal Register, March 5, 1980, p. 14496.

29. Federal Register, January 7, 1981, p. 1910.

30. "Alcohols in Diesel Engines - A Review," Henry Adelman, SAE Paper No. 790956.

31. "A New Way of Direct Injection of Methanol in a Diesel Engine," Franz F. Pischinger and Cornelis Havenith, Paper II-28, Third International Symposium on Alcohol Fuels Technology, May 29-31, 1979, Published by DOE in April 1980.

32. "The Utilization of Different Fuels in a Diesel Engine with Two Separate Injection Systems," P. S. Berg, E. Holmer, and B. I. Bertilsson, Paper II-29, Third Symposium on Alcohol Fuels Technology, May 29-31, 1979, Published by DOE in April 1980.

33. "Alternative Diesel Engine Fuels: An Experimental Investigation of Methanol, Ethanol, Methane, and Ammonia in a D.I. Diesel Engine with Pilot Injection," Klaus Bro and Peter Sunn Pedersen, SAE Paper No. 770794.

34. "Single-Cylinder Engine Evaluation of Methanol-- Improved Energy Economy and Reduced NOx," W. J. Most and J. P. Longwell, SAE Paper No. 750119.

35. "The Alternatives and How to Apply Them to the World Transport Industry," Dr. Winfried Bernhardt, Volkswagen, Second Montreux Energy Forum, May 16-19, 1980.

36. "Emission Characterization of an Alcohol/Diesel-Pilot Fueled Compression-Ignition Engine and Its Heavy-Duty Diesel Counterpart," Terry L. Ullman and Charles T. Hare, Southwest Research Institute, EPA-460/3-81-023, August 1981.

Table 1

Combustion Properties of Different Fuels [1,2,3,4]

Property	Units	Methanol	Gasoline	Diesel
Heating Value	Btu/gallon	57,000	114,000	125,000
	Btu/lb.	8,600	18,000	18,400
Heat of Vaporization	Btu/gallon	3,320	940	880
Vapor Pressure	psi at 38°C	5	6-15	--
Boiling Point	°C	65	30-225	180-330
Flash Point	°C	11	-45	75
Stoichiometric A/F Ratio	lb. air/ lb. fuel	6.4	14.5	14.6
Octane Number	RON	106-110	91-100	30
	MON	90-92	82-90	--
Cetane Number	--	3	0-10	50
Flame Speed	ft./sec.	2.5	1.9	--

CPSIA information can be obtained at www.ICGtesting.com
Printed in the USA
BVOW09s1249100914

366266BV00022B/825/P